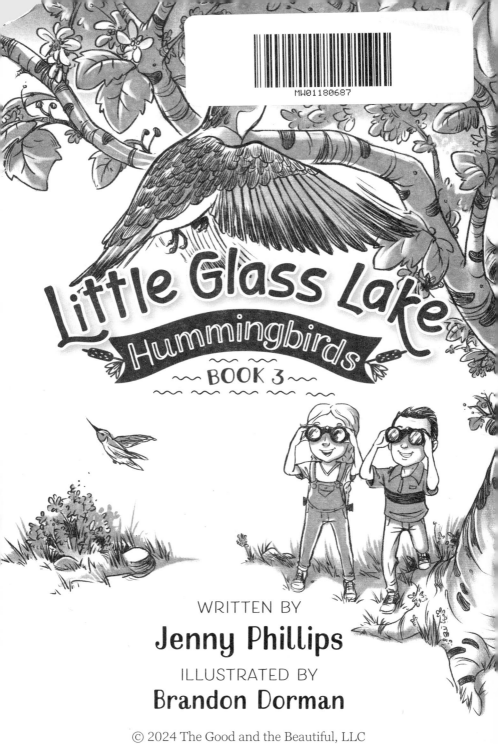

Little Glass Lake
Hummingbirds
~ BOOK 3 ~

WRITTEN BY
Jenny Phillips

ILLUSTRATED BY
Brandon Dorman

TABLE OF CONTENTS

Chapter 1

A blustery June wind swung Holly's braids as she leaned over the garden with a red watering can.

It was ten o'clock in the morning, and Holly could already feel a few beads of sweat on her forehead.

It's going to be a hot day, she thought as she sprinkled water on the thirsty plants.

The driveway to Holly's home was very long. It wound up a gentle hill like a soft ribbon. On one side stood a huge grove of old oak trees that curved around the side of the house and stretched nearly down to Little Glass Lake. Holly loved to walk on the grassy path through the trees, with the green canopy arching above her.

On the other side of the driveway, a large garden

sprawled up the hill. A tall wood-and-metal fence surrounded it to keep out the deer.

After picking a handful of red strawberries, Holly made her way to the top of the garden and sat on a stone bench in the shade of a fruit tree.

This is the perfect spot to watch for Johnny, Holly

thought as she bit into a juicy strawberry.

It had been two weeks since four-year-old Johnny had stayed with Holly's family during his mom's hospital visit. They missed Johnny and were excited when his mom asked if he could spend a couple of hours with Henry and Holly while she had a follow-up appointment with her doctor.

From her viewpoint in the garden, Holly could see the flat stretch of the small lane that ran past their house and then disappeared in both directions over some hills.

Down one of those hills came a big green bike towing a small cart. It was headed directly toward the huge pothole in the lane in front of their house.

I hope he sees it and swerves around it, Holly thought. She watched as the bike came closer, and then she heard the rumble of a large truck from the other direction.

The bike and the truck passed each other on the

lane, causing the bike to hit the pothole with a huge jolt. A large object went flying off the bike's little cart, bouncing twice and landing on the side of the road.

"Hey!" Holly yelled, jumping up from the bench. But the loud noise of the truck drowned out her voice.

Holly kept calling as
the bike disappeared over
the hill. She opened the
garden gate and went

dashing toward the lane, which was now empty and quiet as the truck's rumble faded in the distance.

Holly spotted the object that had fallen off the cart, and she started running toward it. Quickly, she realized that it was a small animal carrier.

Holly suddenly stopped in her tracks. *What kind*

of animal is in there? What if it's hurt from falling off the cart?

Not knowing what to do, Holly looked over her shoulder back to her house. *Should I go get help?*

Sad little whines came from inside the carrier. Holly's heart moved her forward to look into the carrier. The cutest puppy she had ever seen was staring back at her.

Chapter 2

"Oh, are you OK, sweet little puppy?" Holly asked softly.

As if answering, the puppy moved forward, stuck out a little pink tongue, and gave one lick to Holly's hand.

Gently, Holly took hold of the carrier handle

and walked up her driveway, trying not to jiggle the carrier in case the dog was hurt.

"Grandma! Henry!" Holly called as she entered the front door.

"We are in the family room," Grandma Bee called out.

Holly rushed into the room with the carrier and

explained what had just happened out on the lane.

Carefully, Grandma Bee took the dog out of the carrier and inspected her.

"Well, the dog seems fine," Grandma Bee said.

"What should we do with it?" Holly wondered aloud.

Grandma Bee laughed and shook her head. "I'm not sure, but your parents won't be back for a few days, so we'll have to figure something out."

"Look! An address

is taped to the carrier," Henry pointed out.

"Blue Hill Lighthouse Lane," Holly read aloud. "That must be the lane

Deliver to:

34 Blue Hill Lighthouse Lane

that leads up to Blue Hill Lighthouse. We've gone there a few times and walked on the beach."

"Let's look up the address online and see if we can find a phone number that matches it," Grandma Bee suggested as she pulled out her phone.

After a minute she said,

"Hmmm. No name or phone number comes up with that address, but it's only twenty minutes away. We could drive there."

"Great idea!" Holly said.

Just then, the doorbell rang, signaling Johnny's arrival.

"A puppy!" Johnny said as he entered the family room.

"It's a West Highland white terrier—a Westie!" Grandma Bee said. "Someone on Blue Hill Lighthouse

Lane must have ordered her, and the boy on the bike was delivering her."

"Why was the delivery person on a bicycle?" Henry asked. "Wouldn't a car be faster and a lot easier?"

"It wouldn't be as fun!" Holly said with a smile.

Grandma Bee looked up from her phone. "I didn't

find any Westie-breeding companies around here. I can't figure it out. But I'm going to order some groceries to be delivered, and I'll order some puppy dog food too. It'll be here in an hour."

After the puppy food was delivered, Henry poured some into a bowl, and Holly sat watching the puppy eat hungrily.

"Oh no," Holly groaned. "I just thought about the boy pulling the cart with his bike. At some point he probably realized the carrier fell off. He's likely retracing his path to see if he can find the dog. How will he know we have it?"

"We could put a sign

up on the lane," Henry suggested.

Everyone liked the idea, so they worked quickly to make the sign. Then, using duct tape, they attached the sign to a wooden stake and stuck it at the end of their driveway. The sign read, "We have the puppy that fell off the cart."

But they didn't know that the boy with the bicycle had already been back along his whole route and had not seen the puppy, so he had given up.

The sign was too late.

Chapter 3

"I've never seen such a sweet, cute puppy," Holly sighed as she put the white terrier back in her carrier. "I wish we could keep her for a little longer."

"I know," Grandma Bee said lovingly. "But now that Johnny's mom has picked him up, we really should deliver the dog to the address on the carrier."

Holly nodded, and soon she and Henry were with Grandma Bee in the car. Holly put the carrier safely on the floor and then rolled down the window to let the breeze blow gently through the car.

When Grandma Bee tried to start the car, there was a loud, raspy noise for several seconds, followed by loud banging, and then all was quiet.

"What in the world was that?" Grandma Bee exclaimed as she tried to start the car again. But no matter how many times she turned the key, nothing happened.

"The car is broken," Grandma Bee declared. "I suppose I'll have to get a tow truck to take it to a repair shop in town. We'll have to keep the dog a little longer."

"Wahoo!" Holly cried.

Henry put his hand on Holly's shoulder. "But the boy with the bicycle might see the sign and come get the dog, Holly, so don't get too excited."

It was hard for Holly not to get excited. She invited Faith over, and the two friends sat on the couch with the little dog curled up between them.

Grandma Bee sat across the room by the window, reading on her phone about how to care for a terrier puppy. Holly noticed that her cat, Daisy, was curled up on Grandma Bee's lap.

"My cat really likes you, Grandma," Holly noted.

"And I really like her," Grandma Bee replied. "I never thought I liked cats, but she is great company."

Soon the tow truck came. Holly and Faith put the little dog back in the carrier and sat on the front porch while the tow truck loaded the broken-down car.

As the sun sank lower in the sky, Faith told Holly all about Happy Duck Bakery. The building was done, and now they were putting in tables and chairs and decorating. Faith then told Holly about a two-day camp for kids who are blind.

"It has hiking, rafting, swimming, and crafts. Some of my friends are going, and I want to go so much, but it's four hundred fifty dollars! Mom says we don't have any extra money until we get the bakery going."

With all her heart, Holly wished she had four hundred fifty dollars to pay for Faith's camp. Holly had a little pink box in her room where she kept her money, but she only had twelve dollars and fifty-five cents.

Henry came outside with the puppy and a tennis ball. Soon all the children were playing with the puppy. Her mouth was too small to grab the ball, but she loved pushing it along with her nose.

"Come here, Snowball!" Holly called.

"You named the puppy?" Henry exclaimed.

"Yes, I think Snowball is the perfect name," Holly replied.

"You shouldn't get attached to her, Holly,"

Henry warned. "She will be leaving soon."

"I know, but I just love her, and she really looks like a soft snowball," Holly said.

The hum of an electric car drew everyone's attention to the driveway.

Oh no, Holly thought as her heart sank. *It must be the boy looking for the puppy. But I have to try to be happy. The puppy doesn't belong to me.*

The car rolled to a stop, and Holly forced a smile as the car door opened. To her surprise, a very interesting-looking man got out of the car.

Chapter 4

Holly was sure that the man who got out of the car was not the teenager wearing sunglasses and a helmet who had been on the bike. This man was very tall and completely bald, with a long gray mustache.

Grandma Bee, who had

been watching the kids from the window, came out to greet the man.

"How can I help you?" she asked kindly.

He handed her a little card as he spoke. "My name is Dr. Dome. I live two hours away. Someone in this area sketched a picture of a hummingbird they saw in their yard, and

it interests me very much."

Why does a sketch of a hummingbird interest him so much? Holly wondered. But she didn't have to wonder very long.

"I study birds, and I believe that the hummingbird in this sketch is one that hasn't been documented or photographed yet. Keep your eyes open. I wrote the description of the hummingbird on the card I gave you. Anyone who can take a picture of this kind of hummingbird and send it to me will get five hundred dollars."

Excitement rose in Holly. *Five hundred dollars! I could pay for Faith's camp!*

"It won't be easy to get the picture," the man explained, "but please keep a lookout. Let me know even if you just see it."

"We will," Grandma Bee replied.

"I'm going to go get my *Good and Beautiful Animal Guide* on hummingbirds," Holly said after the man drove away in his car.

She returned with the book and settled onto the thick green grass with Faith. Snowball sniffed around nearby as Holly read aloud to Faith. The

girls lost track of time as they marveled at the hummingbird facts.

Grandma Bee called them in to dinner. Holly stood up and looked around. Panic rose up in her as she spun around, scanning the yard.

"Faith! I don't see Snowball anywhere!"

As Holly, Henry, and

Grandma Bee started searching around the yard, Faith called her parents on her phone watch and asked them to come help. She started to call Gabe, too, but then remembered that his family was out of town.

As dusk settled on Little Glass Lake, there was still no sign of Snowball.

Tears pooled in Holly's eyes, making it hard to see in the growing darkness. Henry disappeared into the house and returned with flashlights.

"Henry, you go with Mr. Timms. Holly, you stick right next to me," Grandma Bee said. "We are going to search around the lake."

Mrs. Timms
spoke up. "Faith
and I will wait on
the front porch and let
you know if Snowball
returns."

Soon Holly was deep in
the grove of oak trees with
Grandma Bee. Holly felt
a swoosh above her and
then heard the soft hoot
of an owl.

"Oh, Grandma! Would an owl take Snowball? She's so little," Holly said.

Grandma Bee took a deep breath. "I'm not sure. Let's say a prayer, and then we will keep looking."

Chapter 5

As Holly and Grandma Bee returned to the house, they could see Henry's and Mr. Timms's flashlight beams in the yard.

"It's nearly midnight," Grandma Bee noted when everyone met up. "We can look for Snowball again in the morning, but we should all go to bed now."

Faith gave Holly a tight hug before she left with her parents.

Holly wasn't sure if she had ever been up so late. As worried as she was about Snowball, she fell asleep when her head hit her pillow.

The next morning, Holly slept in late without

meaning to. She woke up with a start and jumped out of bed. Birds flitted past her window, and golden sunlight was pouring into her room, but Holly didn't notice the birds or the sunlight. She was thinking of Snowball.

She ran into the kitchen and slid in her socks across the tile to the counter that Grandma Bee was cleaning.

"Grandma, I have to find Snowball!" Holly exclaimed.

Grandma Bee smiled. "Snowball has been found! She is safe and sound."

"Where is she?" Holly squealed.

Before Grandma Bee

could answer, the doorbell rang.

"Go get the door," Grandma Bee said with a twinkle in her eye.

Holly dashed to the front door and opened it. There stood Gabe holding Snowball.

"Gabe! I thought you were still on your trip," Holly said.

"We came home early last night and found this cute puppy on our porch. We had no idea who it belonged to until this morning, when my dad saw your sign on his way to work. My mom called, and Henry told us all about the puppy."

"Oh! I'm so happy!" Holly gushed, taking

Snowball from Gabe.

"Can you stay and play?"

"Yes! I already asked my mom," Gabe replied.

Holly called Faith to let her know that Snowball had been found. "Can you come over to play?"

"I would love to, but I can't right now," Faith replied. "I am helping my parents get the bakery ready for the grand opening this weekend."

"OK. We will miss you!" Holly said before

ending the call.

"What should we do?"
Gabe asked.

Holly suddenly
remembered the man
who had stopped by their
house. She told Gabe
about the hummingbird,
and they decided to
explore and look for it.

"Oh, I brought this,"
said Gabe, holding up a

leash. "You might want to keep Snowball on this until you take her to her owner."

Grandma Bee walked into the room, holding Daisy. "Speaking of that, the auto repair shop just called. They need to pick up a car part in the next town, so the car won't be fixed until later today."

"Can Snowball come with us to look around for the hummingbird?"

Grandma nodded. "Yes, but keep her on that leash! And remember not to go near the lake."

Chapter 6

As they walked into the shady oak grove, Gabe held Snowball on the leash. Rays of dusty sunlight slanted through the trees.

"Most hummingbird nests are about the size of a ping-pong ball," Holly shared. "The nests are made with small bits of bark, moss, plants, and leaves held together with spiderwebs!"

"Amazing!" Gabe said. "Maybe we should try using spiderwebs as glue sometime."

Holly scrunched up her nose and shook her head. "They would just get stuck all over us!"

"Can you describe the hummingbird we are looking for?" Gabe asked.

Holly pulled the scientist's card from her pocket and read it to Gabe.

"The hummingbird we are looking for has a mint-green head and black beak. The rest of its body is white, except for the wings and tail, which are bright orange."

Gabe stopped and held his finger up to his lips. "Shhhh," he whispered as he pointed to a branch above them. "Look at that tiny bird up there. I think that is what you just described."

With wide eyes, Holly compared the bird to the details on her card.

"It matches perfectly," she whispered just as the bird took flight, darting between some branches. It was quickly out of sight.

Holly and Gabe looked at each other in surprise.

"I can't believe it," Holly said. "How did we find it so fast? If I had just snapped a picture of it, I could've made five hundred dollars!"

"But we don't have a camera," Gabe pointed out.

"Let's go ask my grandma if we can use her phone," Holly said.

Grandma Bee wasn't too excited to let an eight-year-old take her

phone into the grove.
"I'll come with you," she
offered. "It will be fun
being a hummingbird
explorer!"

Holly smiled. "You're
the best, Grandma Bee."

For a long time, the
group quietly searched
through the grove of trees,
but they did not see the
hummingbird again.

"I don't think it's coming back," Gabe said.

Holly sighed. "I think you're right."

Grandma Bee saw how disappointed the children looked, so she made a suggestion. "Why don't you two head up to the tree house, and I'll bring out a picnic lunch."

"Great idea!" Holly said.

The two friends
scrambled up the ladder to
the tree house. Grandma
Bee and Snowball walked

to the house and returned a short time later with lunch.

"Here comes the bucket," Holly called down to Grandma Bee. "Watch your head!"

Holly pulled on the rope that lowered the bucket down. Grandma Bee loaded it with all the lunch goodies.

"OK, Holly. Pull it back up!" Grandma Bee called out.

"May I pull it?" Gabe asked. He was fascinated by the pulley system that raised and lowered the bucket.

"Sure," Holly replied as she handed the rope to Gabe.

They chatted away as

they ate and kept a lookout
for the hummingbird.

"I should ask Grandma
Bee to call Dr. Dome.
He said to contact him
even if we just saw the
hummingbird. But I still
hope I can get a picture
of it. I really want the
five-hundred-dollar
reward."

"What would you do with all that money?" Gabe asked.

Holly told Gabe about the camp that Faith wanted so badly to go to.

"I hope she can go too," Gabe said. "We've got to find that hummingbird again!"

As the kids finished their lunch, a gusty wind

picked up, swaying the big branches of the oak tree above them.

"Those are some very dark and mean-looking clouds," Holly observed.

Just then, Grandma Bee called from the ground below. "There's a big thunderstorm rolling in, kids. It's expected to pack quite a punch, and a flash flood watch was just issued for this area. It's time to come down and get inside."

The children quickly bounded down the ladder. Gabe hurried home, and Holly held Grandma Bee's hand as they rushed toward the house.

Inside they found Henry in the family room

reading *The Bronze Bow* on the big beanbag chair, with Snowball curled up on the floor beside him.

"This storm is moving in fast," Grandma Bee said as she sat down on the couch next to Daisy. The cat stretched and yawned and climbed onto Grandma Bee's lap.

Holly plopped down on

the couch. "Do you think the little hummingbird will be OK in this storm?"

Grandma Bee pulled out her phone and started looking up hummingbird facts. "It says here that

they can fly in the rain. In fact, they don't mind light rain at all. They have oil on their feathers that helps repel water. But during heavy rain, hummingbirds usually find shelter."

Just then, the tinkling of rain sounded on the roof, and Grandma Bee's phone rang. She left the room and came back shortly.

"My car is fixed! Mrs. Timms is taking me into town to pick it up. Then we can deliver Snowball to Blue Hill Lighthouse Lane."

Holly felt a lump in her throat and looked down at the little sleeping ball of fur. *I don't have much more time with you, little girl.*

Chapter 7

Shortly after Grandma Bee left, the dark, mean-looking pile of clouds reached their home.

Buckets of rain gushed out of the sky, splashing on the roof so fast that the gutters couldn't catch it all. Water poured off the sides of the house as if it were beneath a waterfall.

Snowball woke up and started whining. Holly patted the dog gently and then turned to look out the window. She saw that the driveway had turned into a little stream, with water running down the hill.

Suddenly, the pounding

on the roof got very loud, and Holly saw spots of white bouncing everywhere on the ground outside.

"It's hail!" Holly shouted to Henry. "Come and see."

Soon the ground was covered in a layer of white.

"It looks like snow," Henry noted.

By the time Grandma Bee returned, the hail had turned back to rain, but it was still coming down hard.

"Oh, it's cold and wet out there!" Grandma Bee said as she brushed the rain from her hair. "Some of the low spots on the road are flooded. I don't think it's a good idea to deliver Snowball tonight."

More time with Snowball! Holly cheered inside.

All night and into the next morning, the rain pattered steadily on the roof.

Holly's brown eyes blinked open, but she stayed in her cozy bed, watching water droplets slide down the window.

Maybe Snowball will get to stay another day since it's still raining, she thought.

After her chores, Holly read picture books to Snowball, who barked at the page at times, making Holly laugh.

Grandma Bee called out from the kitchen,

"Lunchtime!"

Holly dropped the book

onto the window seat and clapped her hands at Snowball. "You hear that, girl? It's time to eat! Are you hungry?"

Snowball danced around Holly's feet, wagging her tail and barking happily.

"Let's go have some lunch," Holly said as she skipped out of her room.

Snowball followed close behind.

"Pigs in a blanket!" Grandma Bee said. "I wanted to make you something fun for lunch."

As Holly and Henry ate the hot dogs wrapped in flaky, golden-brown crescent rolls, Grandma Bee told them that she had called Dr. Dome to let him know that Holly and Gabe had seen the hummingbird. "He's excited but hesitant. He wonders if you two saw the right bird."

"Oh, we did!" Holly claimed.

"I think you probably did, but Dr. Dome still wants to have a picture of it. If it's around here, I'm sure you will see it again."

Grandma Bee's phone buzzed. She answered it and then frowned as she listened. "Oh dear, yes, we will be right over."

Grandma Bee hung up the phone. "The river that flows past Gabe's house and into Little Glass Lake is flooding. They need our help."

Chapter 8

"How can we help with a river flooding?" Holly asked.

"Water usually goes wherever it wants to," Henry chimed in.

"Sandbags!" Grandma Bee explained as she put on her jacket.

As they drove the short

distance to Gabe's house, the rain continued to pound on the car. Holly stared out the window and wondered where the hummingbird with orange wings was. She hoped it was safe from all this rain.

When they pulled into Gabe's driveway, Holly could see the little river by Gabe's big barn. The water had risen to the top of the banks.

In the barn they found Mr. Timms and a few other people already helping fill sandbags. Holly got right to work, holding bags open while Henry used a shovel to fill them with sand. It seemed to Holly that they had been filling bags for hours

when Gabe's dad finally
announced that they had
enough.

It wasn't safe for Holly
to go by the swelling,

swift-moving little river. She couldn't lift the sandbags anyway, so she watched from the barn window as the others stacked the sandbags on top of each other along the curve of the river that went past Gabe's house.

Holly, Henry, and Grandma Bee were invited to stay for a late dinner,

but Grandma Bee felt
they needed to get back to
make sure Snowball was
doing OK.

After getting all cleaned

up, Holly half fell asleep while eating. She had worked hard helping with the sandbags. It was only eight o'clock when she snuggled into bed and listened to the rain drumming on the roof. *Drum-drum-drum-drum.*

And she quickly fell asleep.

Chapter 9

Holly lay in bed for a moment after opening her eyes. *I don't hear rain,* she thought. *I hear birds!*

She hopped out of bed and went to the window. After all the rain, the sunlight streaming across her yard was dazzling. It glinted and glittered on

the wet grass.
Holly got dressed
and went to the garden
to pick strawberries

for breakfast, Snowball following along at her heels. Holly giggled as she watched Snowball chase a yellow butterfly.

The plants were pearled with raindrops. Holly breathed in deeply. The air carried the fresh smell of the world right after rain.

After breakfast Holly found Grandma Bee

folding laundry in the laundry room. Daisy was sitting on the counter right next to her.

"Did Gabe's house flood?" Holly asked.

"No," Grandma Bee reported. "The sandbags saved the day!"

Holly chewed her lip as she watched her grandma work.

She's doing so much for us, Holly thought. *I want to do something to help her.*

Holly wandered into the kitchen and saw the breakfast dishes piled in the sink. *That's how I can help!* Holly realized.

She dragged a chair over to the sink and turned on the water. Humming happily, Holly started washing the dishes. She was enjoying the sound of water filling the sink when she suddenly looked up at the window.

Was that a flash of orange? Holly stared out the window. Another quick flash caught her eye. *Oh! It was. It's the hummingbird!*

The little bird darted from one flower to another on the bush outside the kitchen window.

Holly turned off the water and jumped down from the chair to find Grandma Bee.

"It's here! It's here!" she called out as she ran through the house.

"What is?" Henry asked, poking his head out the doorway of his room.

"The hummingbird!" Holly exclaimed. "Quick, Grandma, grab your phone!"

Grandma Bee and Henry followed Holly excitedly.

"There it is!" Henry

whispered, pointing by the kitchen window.

Grandma Bee saw the beautiful, tiny bird with the mint-colored head, the black beak, the white body, and the orange wings and tail. "You're right, Holly! This is just as Dr. Dome described the bird! Hurry, take some pictures."

As Holly snapped pictures using her grandma's phone, they realized that the bird had built a nest right under the kitchen window.

Grandma Bee could barely contain her excitement. As soon as Holly passed the phone back, Grandma Bee called Dr. Dome. "My granddaughter found the hummingbird, and it's building a nest under our kitchen window!"

Grandma Bee then texted Dr. Dome the pictures. As soon as he saw them, he said he would be there in two hours.

Grandma Bee hung up the phone and turned to Holly. "I'm so sorry, dear, but we really should deliver Snowball to the address on the carrier now. We have time to go and come back before Dr. Dome gets here."

"OK," Holly said sadly.

Chapter 10

As they drove through the hills with the windows down, Holly breathed in the fresh air and marveled at the huge puddles left by the rainstorm.

Soon Holly smelled salt in the air. "We're getting close to the ocean."

"Yes, we are," Grandma

Bee agreed. "In fact, we are now on the peninsula that goes out to the lighthouse."

"I just learned about peninsulas," Holly said. "They're areas of land that have water on three sides."

"What's going on up ahead?" Henry asked.

Grandma Bee slowed down and came to a stop.

A little farther down the road, a big tractor was in the middle of the road, lifting its huge shovel. Police lights were flashing.

A police officer walked toward them and stopped by Grandma Bee's window. "Blue Hill Lighthouse Lane is closed. The rain caused a mudslide onto the road.

We are working on it now and hope to have it open by tomorrow afternoon."

As Grandma Bee turned the car around, Holly felt confused. *I'm excited to have more time with Snowball, but it's also getting harder and harder to think about parting with her.*

"I don't think we are

ever going to be able to return this dog!" Henry said.

Grandma Bee laughed. "It sure seems like it! Your parents will be home this afternoon, so they can help you bring the dog to her owner. For now, let's stop by Happy Duck Bakery. It opens this weekend, and Mrs.

Timms invited us to be taste testers!"

Soon they were sinking their teeth into dream puffs.

"What is in this? It's amazing!" Holly raved.

Mrs. Timms smiled. "It's my own recipe. It's a pastry puff filled with white chocolate fluff and raspberry cream, dipped

in a caramel sauce,
and sprinkled with
white chocolate shavings."

"Don't forget the best part, Mom," Faith added. "The pastry dough is made with duck eggs!"

After taste testing, Holly and her family had to hurry home. They pulled into the driveway just before Dr. Dome did. *Oh no, what if the hummingbird is not there anymore?* Holly thought.

But it was, and Dr. Dome was very excited to see it. Out of his bag, he pulled five one-hundred-dollar bills and handed them to Holly.

With big, round eyes, Holly looked at the money. "Wow, thank you!"

After Dr. Dome took more pictures, he turned

to Grandma Bee. "It's incredible that you all found this hummingbird. It's even more incredible that it is building a nest right outside your kitchen window. Would you consider allowing me to set up a live cam to show the nest to the world?"

"What's a live cam?" Holly asked.

"It's a little camera that we would install near the nest," Dr. Dome replied. "It doesn't disturb the hummingbird at all, but it would stay on all the time so that anyone can get on the Internet and watch the nest. Because this is a newly discovered bird, many people all over the world will want the chance to watch and study it."

"That would be so cool!" Henry exclaimed. "Right here at our home!"

After Grandma Bee called Holly's parents and got permission, Dr. Dome practically ran to his car to get his equipment. Henry and Holly followed him to the front of the house.

As Holly rounded the corner, she stopped in her tracks. A green bike was coming up the driveway.

Chapter 11

"Hello!" the teenage boy said as he hopped off the bike. "I saw your sign about the dog."

Henry shook the boy's hand and explained all the delays they had faced.

"That's OK," the boy said. "I'm just glad to know that the dog is safe.

My name is Grady. I was
delivering the puppy to
my grandpa when the

carrier fell off my cart. Pets can really bring a lot of comfort to people who live alone."

"We're sorry we've had her all this time," Holly said.

Grandma Bee came out onto the front porch with Snowball on the leash.

"That's OK," the boy answered. "Our dog had

two puppies, so we gave my grandpa the other one. We'll find a home for this one."

Holly gasped and reached down to scoop up Snowball. "*I* want her!"

"Well," the boy glanced around at everyone, "you see, we sell our dogs. She's purebred."

"I could buy her. I have

twelve dollars and fifty-five cents in a pink box in my room," Holly offered. "How much does she cost?"

Grady looked a little sad. "A lot more than that, I'm afraid. She is five hundred dollars."

"Oh," Holly mumbled. "That's a lot."

After considering the

options for a few seconds, Holly reluctantly handed Snowball to Grady.

"Thank you, but I don't have that much money to spend," she said as tears welled up in her eyes.

Henry looked confused. "What do you mean, Holly? What about the money Dr. Dome gave you?"

"I can't use it," Holly said sadly. "I promised myself that if I got the money for the picture, I would give it to Faith so she could go to her camp."

Holly turned and ran to the backyard, wiping away the tears that fell. She sat down on the porch steps to watch Dr. Dome install his camera, hoping that would take her mind off having to give up Snowball.

"There you are," said a familiar voice a few minutes later. "We've been looking for you."

Holly looked up to see her parents walking around the corner of the house.

Chapter 12

"You're back!" Holly shouted, running to her parents. "I've missed you!"

"We've missed you too," Holly's mom said as she wrapped Holly in a hug.

Holly's dad spoke up. "Tell us all about what you've been up to."

Henry and Grandma
Bee joined the rest of the
family on the back porch,
where they all shared

stories of things they had done. Henry told them about the big storm that almost flooded Gabe's house, and Holly told them about Snowball's falling off the cart and getting to take care of her.

"What about him?" Holly's dad asked, pointing at Dr. Dome. "Grandma Bee has told us a little about how he ended up installing a camera, but I'd love to hear the details from you."

So Holly and Henry spent the next few minutes sharing all the details, from Dr. Dome's first appearance in their driveway to why he was setting up the camera.

Dr. Dome walked up
just as they finished. "I
can't tell you how grateful
I am that you've allowed
me to set up the live
cam," he said as he

shook hands with Holly's dad. "Everything is installed, so I'll be on my way. I've got a long drive ahead."

"Me too," Grandma Bee said. "I'm going to pack up." As Grandma Bee turned to go into the house, she petted Daisy lovingly and said, "I'm going to miss you, Daisy."

Holly suddenly remembered what Grady had said: "Pets can really bring a lot of comfort to people who live alone."

Grandma Bee and Daisy have a wonderful bond, Holly thought.

"Grandma, I want you to take Daisy home with you!" Holly said.

Grandma Bee turned

around. "But she's your pet, Holly. I can't take your pet."

"I do love Daisy, but I have Henry and Mom and Dad here to keep me company. You live all by yourself. Daisy loves you, and she could keep you company." Holly paused and looked at her parents. "Is that OK, Mom and

Dad?" Holly asked.

Holly's parents looked at each other and smiled. Then Mom nodded to Holly. "If you're sure, then, yes, it's OK with us."

Grandma Bee hugged Holly. "You are such a thoughtful girl. I will take very good care of Daisy and bring her back with me the next time I

visit. Thank you!"

"You're welcome, Grandma," Holly replied.

LITTLE GLASS LAKE: BOOK 3

Henry and Holly stayed on the porch talking while the others went back inside.

"Aren't you sad, Holly?" Henry asked.

"Yes and no," Holly said. "I will really miss Daisy, but I have such a nice feeling in my heart right now. It seems that nothing could be greater

than the way I feel. I
can picture Grandma in
the evenings with Daisy
curled up in her lap,
keeping her company, and
it makes me so happy."

Henry nodded. "It
makes me happy too. And
it makes me happy to have
you as my sister."

Holly's heart felt so
full she thought it might

burst. As she entered the back door to her house and walked into the kitchen, she was nearly knocked over by a little white ball of fur.

"Snowball!" Holly cried, kneeling down to pick up the dog. "I thought you went with Grady. Why are you here?"

"Because I bought her for you," Grandma Bee declared with a big smile.

"You did?" Holly beamed.

Grandma Bee nodded. "Yes, I did."

"Oh, thank you so much, Grandma!" Holly exclaimed.

Holly smiled. Holly's mom and dad smiled.

Henry and Grandma Bee smiled. Even Little Glass Lake seemed to be smiling as the sunlight shone on the smooth water and on a little mint-headed hummingbird that was flying by.

Continue the adventures with book 4 of the Little Glass Lake series!

Little Glass Lake Rabbits
By Jenny Phillips

goodandbeautiful.com

Check out these other Level 2B books from The Good and the Beautiful!

Mary Helen and the Black Pony

By Molly Taylor Sanchez

Maria's Many Kittens

By Breckyn Wood

goodandbeautiful.com